ONCE UPON A STAGE
Story-based Creative Dramatics with Young Children

CHRISTMAS

To my parents, who still don't quite understand what I do, but think it's great anyway, and to my best friend, Lisa, who never minds sharing her brain to help me do it

–R.G.

To my grandmother, Mary Etta Strong, who loved to tell the story

–D.S.

Table of Contents

Table of Contents

Once Upon a Stage combines a leader's guide, creative exercises, organizer and scripts in one easy-to-use resource for producing short plays with children ages 4-10. This volume offers information useful for any children's dramatics program, together with three short scripts for simple plays suitable for Advent and Christmas.

Who will enjoy working with this book? Anyone who wants to try imaginative story-based activities with young children, but especially:

★ day-care providers
★ leaders of after-school programs
★ parochial school teachers
★ catechists
★ Sunday school teachers
★ anyone wanting guidance in producing a simple Christmas play starring young children as the performers

In the first section of the book—"Getting Started"—you'll find information on setting up a creative dramatics program. First we give advice on how to structure the program as a whole, then share a few games we have found useful in helping children release energy and focus their attention on the tasks at hand. We also give advice on how to choose a play that will hold the interest of your group.

The second section of the book—"Doing the Work"—gives easy-to-follow directions for making a play from one of three starting points: your own imagination, a familiar story or a play script. We also give tips for how to keep your production both simple and satisfying.

The third section of the book—"Scripts"—gives one possible Christmas play for each of the three starting points described in "Doing the Work." Choose from:

★ a quick improvisation based on a familiar Christmas carol
★ a longer story built on a picture book of the Nativity story
★ a full-fledged script based on a popular Advent devotion that ties the gospel story of Jesus' birth to its Old Testament roots

We've included tips, diagrams and record forms throughout to make your task even easier. You'll find additional space for notes on pages 70-74. We hope you and the children you lead enjoy a time together devoted to imagination, self-expression and cooperation. See you onstage!

How to Structure a Creative Dramatics Program

In any program, it's always good to establish a daily routine that the children will recognize. Divide your session into segments—a warm-up segment, a games segment and a "work" segment. Some of the games, and even some of the warm-ups, will relate to the work, depending on the nature of your production.

In the beginning, you'll want to have a long warm-up, a shorter games period and an even shorter work period. (In fact, the first few sessions may be more productive as sessions devoted to warm-up and games only, dividing the time between them roughly half and half.)

As time goes on, increase the games period to half the session, with the warm-up and work periods taking up approximately one-quarter of your time each. Gradually increase the work periods and decrease the games.

As the performance date draws near, eliminate the games, and add another section to the session: review. The younger the children, the more review you need. Make certain you leave time at the end of each session to reinforce and practice old material, or you will soon find the old material turning back into new material.

Tip:
Especially if you are planning a public performance, there will be a strong temptation to skip over the warm-up and just get to work. This is nearly always a mistake. Never skip the warm-up, ever. Not even on the day of performance. *Especially* not on the day of performance. The warm-up is what triggers ingrained habits of behavior, so don't be surprised if the day you decide to skimp on warm-up is the day everyone forgets his or her lines.

Schedule for a
Creative Dramatics Program

If you are building toward the performance of a short play, when will that performance be?

Date:_____

How many weeks are there between now and that date?

Number of weeks:_____

How many regular sessions do you expect to lead between now and the performance of the play? (Multiply the number of weeks in your program by the number of sessions in each week.) For example:

> 12 (weeks in the program) x 2 (sessions per week) = 24 (sessions in the program)

Number of sessions in the program:_____

How would you like to divide the work between these sessions? Record your notes and ideas below. We recommend:

★ first 2-3 sessions devoted to warm-up and play selection

★ review work included in the last 1/4 of the program

★ when possible, extra rehearsal sessions directly preceding the play

_____

_____

_____

_____

_____

_____

_____

_____

Notes

How to Structure a Creative Dramatics Session
Warm-ups

An actor's primary tools are his body and his voice. Both need warming up. Even with children as young as four, warm-ups are beneficial. The point of a warm-up is to release excess energy, and then focus the attention. You will then be able to use that focus to work.

Step One: Release Energy

Children have astounding amounts of energy, and often no way to release it, especially in structured settings, such as schools or day-care centers. Making young children sit still for a long period of time is almost impossible—and so it should be. Give them a chance to move, instead. The best way to start a session is to offer a way to release that pent-up energy with a few minutes of explosive activity.

Energy releasers:
★ Tag (especially group tag that gets everyone running)
★ races
★ screaming (cover your ears and bear it; you'll be happy when you see how much 15 seconds of free yelling yields you in attention span)
★ physical exercise (jumping jacks, etc.)

These are just suggestions—most games popular with children involve the right elements. Pick one they like, and let them—*go!*

Step Two: Focus Attention

Use focus games to grab the attention immediately after the energy releaser. Don't let these games drag on too long, and don't make them so complicated that they feel like work. You merely want to get everyone paying attention and thinking together.

Focus exercises:
★ Follow the Leader: One child leads a line of children around the room. The children who follow mimic every movement of the leader.
★ Mirrors: Children in pairs mimic a mirror as they try to match each other's movements exactly.
★ Simon Says: *Simon* tells children what to do, showing each movement ordered. The other children copy the movements if the order begins with *Simon Says;* they ignore all other orders.
★ Rhythm Games: Children can try to match a rhythm made with claps of the hand, slaps to the thighs, finger snaps, etc.
★ Freeze: Children move freely until a leader calls "Freeze!" They hold their position as still as possible until the leader releases them.

Tip:
Try a few games, but when you find one that works, stick with it. The goal is to train behaviors and ways of thinking. It will take time, but eventually when you say "Simon says hands up" or clap a certain rhythm, the children will naturally fall into "work mode."

Tip:

Try to end each session on a positive note, with a game that everyone enjoyed or a scene that worked. If something goes especially well, it's better to stop a few minutes early and leave everyone in a good mood than try to squeeze an extra five minutes of work in.

The Best Focus Game Ever

This is a game we find highly successful with younger children. It's not to be used in place of focus exercises, but is highly effective as the last thing you do just before you begin serious work. We call it Alien, but you can make up any story you like about it.

Here's the story as Randi tells it the first time:

I am an alien, and this is my garden. I love statues. I collect statues, but I zap people with my ray gun. You don't want to get zapped. The only way I can tell people from statues is that people move, and statues don't. So if you don't want to get zapped, don't move!

Then Randi usually does a little speech about how statues don't talk, laugh, stick their tongues out, etc., but they do breathe, and occasionally sneeze or cough. Sounds silly, but children can take you very literally if you're not careful!

Next Randi (as the Alien) turns around and counts to ten. When she turns back around, she "zaps" anyone that moves, and that per-

son is "out." The game continues until she zaps everyone except one, and that person is the winner.

Children love this game! They try to stay still as long as they can. Not only does a daily game increase attention span over time, it gives them a reference point for understanding *how* to stay still. ("Now we all have to stand very quietly—just as if we were playing Alien.")

Focusing the Voice

Young children are notorious for speaking in either a whisper or a shout as soon as they get on stage. Teach them *early* the difference between projecting and screaming.

One to Ten is a great game for practicing use of the voice. Choose a short phrase—anything will do, so long as it is short enough not to tax memory. Try "I love drama class" or "We're putting on a play."

Ask everyone to repeat the phrase. Vary the volume, making sure to correct both whispers and screams—you want to encourage *speaking* loudly and *speaking* softly.

Say the number "five" at a normal speaking tone. Ask everyone to say the phrase at "five," then "six," and so on, all the way up to "ten." Then go back down to "one" and back up to "ten" once again. Get everyone used to the idea that they can project their voices at any level they choose.

Next, skip around, try to trick the children and make them laugh by saying "four" when they expect you to say "ten." This will teach them to pay attention and think before they respond.

End the game by saying, "Ready? One!" and going straight from one to ten. In time, the "ready" will signal to them that you're going straight through.

This game takes a bit of time to develop—the children may not be able to go consistently from one to ten the first time, or even the first twelve times. But it is an invaluable exercise, because it provides a frame of reference—when someone onstage whispers, you can say, "That was a two, now say the line as an eight" and they will understand!

Tip:
When you finally have the attention of your group, you will definitely want to know what to do next. Planning ahead is essential. Pick a couple of "emergency back-up games" that you can always fall back on if you need to take a few minutes to gather your thoughts.

Games Log

Record below the games you use and how well they work. Which games best help the children in the group release energy before turning to structured work? Which games best help the children concentrate on working together on tasks?

Energy releasers: _____

_____

_____

Focus games: _____

_____

_____

7

How to Choose a Play

Many elements go into play selection, but the most important question to ask yourself is, "Do I like it?" Never choose a piece that doesn't appeal strongly to you in some way. You will be spending an enormous amount of time with this piece over the next few weeks or even months. If you don't like it at the start, you'll wish you had never heard of it by the time rehearsals are halfway done.

Other elements to consider in choosing a play are cast size, limitations on budget or construction possibilities, copyright decisions, and the sometimes-conflicting tastes of actors and audience.

Cast Size

How many people are in your group? If you need parts for fifteen children, don't pick a three-person play. Sounds simple enough, right? Wrong. You also need to think about *cast breakdown*.

How many boys do you have? How many girls? Don't assume that because the part is written for a boy, it has to be played by one. In many cases you can change John to Jane with a minimum of fuss. (Biblical plays espe-

Tip:

Make sure you think about scene changes. Maybe you *can* build the castle exterior and the princess's chambers and the throne room, but how will you switch back and forth between the scenes? Don't choose something that will require major scene changes if you don't have the personnel to do them, and the backstage space to store them!

cially need to be cast with flexibility. There's no reason girls can't be angels, shepherds or innkeepers.) Consider that as you read.

How many speaking parts are there? How many large parts? Is there an ensemble of townspeople for the shy contingent? This is where it becomes vital that you know your group. Choosing *Cinderella* can lead to a dead end if you have no one to play the Prince.

How many children in the group actually want to speak in the play? How many will panic if they're pulled to the front and would be better off simply as trees?

Make a list that breaks down the characters into:
★ principals
★ supporting roles
★ non-speaking or minor roles

Break down this list further into male or female parts, remembering as above that most roles could be played by either. (Nonetheless you'll be better off with a girl as Mary and a boy as Joseph.)

Now you have a place to start.

Budget and Construction Requirements

Read through the potential scripts and make a list of scenes, major costumes and major set pieces. Consider the overall picture, and at the same time look for expensive or difficult items. Remember, you can't do *Sleeping*

Beauty without a spinning wheel. Is one in your budget? Can you borrow one? Will you be happy with one made from cardboard? Do you have someone to make that for you— even from cardboard? If the answer to these questions is "no," go on to another script.

A Word about Royalties

All published plays, unless they are in the public domain, have royalties attached to them. (The scripts in this book are an exception. If you purchased this book, you have our permission to perform any of the three plays, without paying royalties, provided you keep to the guidelines described on the copyright and permissions page.)

Do not assume that because a piece is very old it is in the public domain. Do not assume that because you are a non-profit organization, or putting on your play for free, you do not have to pay royalties. Often you do.

Call the publisher listed in whatever version of the piece you have. If they don't own the rights, they will know who does. The owner of the rights will ask you some questions (How many performances are you having? How many seats are in your house? What are your ticket prices?) and then quote you a per-show rate. Often the first show is more expensive, and additional performances less.

Don't be afraid to plead poverty, or write a letter explaining your non-profit status. Often publishers will reduce or waive royal-

ties if you ask. But you must ask! Do not simply assume that you are exempt—putting on a show without permission is both illegal and risky. The last thing you need is a 'cease and desist' order on opening day because you tried to save a few dollars and some-one's uncle happens to work for the pub-lisher. It has been known to happen that way.

Players and Audiences

Next to your own enjoyment of the play chosen, the en-joyment of the chil-dren you lead is crit-ical to the success of the play. Will the children like the show? Will they un-derstand it? If you like it and they hate it, the experience will be unpleasant all around. Try to choose a play with plenty of action and a limited amount of dialogue if you have younger children.

Consider the needs of your audience, too. A short Christmas play performed only for the parents of the actors is bound to please no matter what. Few audiences could be less

Tip:
Copyright laws apply also to well-known interpretations of public domain works. For ex-ample, Disney owns the rights to its versions of fairy-tale characters. If you want to do *Snow White* with dwarves named Dopey, Sleepy or Doc, you need Disney's permission *even if you write your own script.*

9

critical. Still, many shows for children are written to appeal to adult audiences as well. Often there are jokes which the actors don't necessarily understand, but the audience members do. In one script that we provide—*The Jesse Tree*—biblical references are chosen to provoke and maintain adult interest. Try to strike a balance by finding a play that the children will like and the adults won't snore through.

Play Choice

Use this checklist as you consider a play for the group.

How many children will participate?_____

How many parts are in this play? Speaking parts? Large parts?_____

_____

_____

What costumes, sets and props will we need?_____

_____

_____

Does this play meet our limitations of budget? Of time?_____

_____

Will royalties be required?_____

Does this play appeal to me? To the children? To the expected audience?_____

_____

_____

_____

How to Make a Play from Scratch

Suppose you want to create your own play. For one reason or the other, you just haven't found any story that meets all your needs. Well, never fear. You can write your own.

You really need only the most basic understanding of play structure to do this. Most plays are put together in the same way; they move from balance to interruption to conflict.

The play begins with a situation in balance: Cinderella is miserable and badly treated, but cannot do anything about it. The King and Queen are showing off their darling new baby. A young girl decides to take a basket of goodies to her grandmother's house.

Something happens near the beginning which upsets the balance and creates a conflict: An invitation to the prince's ball arrives. An evil fairy curses the baby to sleep for a hundred years. A wolf spies the little girl in the forest and decides to eat her.

The action of the play explores and concludes the conflict: The Prince rescues Cinderella from her unhappy life. The Prince kisses Sleeping Beauty and breaks the curse. A huntsman destroys the wolf and rescues the girl and her grandmother.

In fairy tales, the newly-created balance is generally expressed as, "They lived happily ever after," and this is almost always the right conclusion to any play for young children, too. (Early Christians understood this dynamic very well. They never told the story of Jesus' crucifixion without the concluding story of his resurrection.)

Before you try to create your own play, choose some other stories and try to unravel their structures.

Now choose a general setting for your piece. Say you want a Christmas story—there are unlimited possibilities, such as:
★ Christmas morning in an orphanage
★ Christmas eve in a family's house in Wisconsin
★ The week before Christmas in a toy store
★ A manger in Jerusalem (This is the one we use in *Come to Bethlehem* on page 40.)

For example, let's choose the next-to-the-last situation: the week before Christmas in a toy store. Now you can work the same way you would begin if you had a story. The challenge is, of course, that this time you and the children need to create the characters yourselves, instead of merely identifying them in the story. Start with the question, "Who is usually in a toy store?" Make a list:
★ the people who work there
★ the customers
★ the toys! (Characters don't have to be people.)

Next ask, "Who else would come to the toy store on an average day?" Add to your list:

★ the postman
★ delivery people

Discuss with your group the specifics of the characters. How many are there? Who are they?

When you have created a basic cast of characters and defined their basic relationships, you have created a balanced situation—some people are working in the store, others are shopping, etc.

Perhaps you've decided upon a mother and daughter buying gifts for the rest of their family. Maybe there is a father who is trying to select the right toys for his children. Possibly one of the clerks is trying to get everything done so she can go home early, but cranky customers, rushed with last-minute shopping, give her a hard time with unreasonable requests.

Now you need to interrupt this balanced situation with a conflict. What could go wrong here?

★ Two customers want the same toy and there is only one.
★ Two children start making noise in the store because they can't find their parent.
★ The clerk who needs to leave gets locked in the stockroom.

There are dozens of other possibilities. With the help of the children, brainstorm some of these possibilities. Together choose one.

Your task for the rest of your play is to get from the interruption back to a balance. What are some possible routes to that happy ending?

★ Toys come alive on the shelves, appealing to the customers to take them home.
★ Customers trade original picks for new ones, and a child whom everyone had been ignoring gets the argued-over toy.

The toys played and danced together.

When Mr. Murphy saw the toys he shouted "WONDERFUL!"

★ The children ask customers and store workers to help find their parent. They look in many silly places—inside the cash register, behind the Nintendo sets—before finding him oblivious to the commotion of the search because he is reading a book. Choose an older child as the parent, and you can have the book turn out to be a simple Christmas tale that the parent reads aloud to his children. (And to the audience, of course.) This book could be written by the children themselves, and illustrated on sheets of poster board, bound together with thick yarn.

★ All the customers try to get the clerk out by using different toys to rescue them. Working together to rescue the clerk reminds the clerk and customers both that the real point of a holiday is enjoying the people around us.

Once you have the basic story invented, read the next session to find out "How to Make a Play from a Story." Some of the possibilities we've described above will work best with children at least seven or eight years old. For a play from scratch that will work with preschoolers and kindergartners, turn to page 40 and read *Come to Bethlehem*.

How to Make a Play from a Story

Note: Some of the ideas discussed in this section are based loosely on the techniques of Winifred Ward, a pioneer in story drama.

The three stages in every story drama session are: explain, enact, evaluate. With any work period, you need to first explain the task, then enact the task, then evaluate the results together. *Do not* skip the evaluation step, as tempting as that might be—that's when actors learn.

Work Sessions

Once you have chosen a story, you're ready for the first three-part work session of explain, enact and evaluate. Tell the children what story you have chosen and why. Explain that together you're going to take this story and turn it into a play.

Then enact: read the story aloud. If you are using a picture book, allow plenty of time to show the pictures to the children. Let the group simply listen to a good story.

Finally evaluate: discuss the story as a story. Start with basic questions, useful for any book talk with children:

★ What did you like about the story?

★ What is the story about?

★ What questions do you wish you could ask the writer about this story?

Depending on your time frame, you can stop there or continue. Continue *only* if you have enough time to run all three steps again. It's better to stop early than be interrupted in the middle. With all these steps, go as far as you want, and leave the rest until next time. Just remember to never skip evaluation.

Characters

A good place to start your next session or sessions is with characters. Explain:

★ I'm going to read the story again.

★ As you listen, think about the people (or *animals, toys, etc.)* in the story.

★ Who are they? What are they like? *(Discourage discussion at this point. First you want them to listen again.)*

Then enact: read the story again. You may wish to read it straight through, or you may wish to stop and discuss each character as she appears. You will know the attention span and story retention skills of the children.

Start with the character who has the most clearly defined relationships with the people around her. Ask:

★ Who is the most important person (*animal, toy, etc.*) in the story?

★ How old do you think this person is?

★ Would you like to be friends with this person? Why or why not?

★ What could this person eat? Do? Wear?

Draw (or invite a volunteer to draw) a picture of the character on chalkboard, newsprint or poster board. Label the drawing with the character's name. This will help everyone to keep track of the cast. Discuss clothing and write ideas down to use later in planning costumes. When you use a picture book, some of this character work is pre-empted. Try not to let the children rely too much on the artist's conception of the character, so that the children's own imaginations are engaged.

When you're ready to move on to another character, begin by finding the new character's relationship to the first character. In other words, rather than beginning with "John is a forty-year-old man," begin with "John is Ann's father."

Defining characters can take a single session or several. Use your judgement. Concentrate on how the characters feel about each other. Do they like each other? What activities would they do together?

Once the cast list—a group of drawings—is made, go back to the beginning of the process. Explain:

★ Now that we know the characters, let's listen to the story again.

★ As I read, listen especially to information about the characters we discussed.

★ Think about whether you hear anything new about these characters.

Tip:
It's easy to spend too much time on the physical appearance of the characters, but this is a trap. Don't forget that you are using this process to build a *play*. Eventually the children will portray these characters, and you may run into problems if the actors do not look like the characters they have imagined. Avoid creating a situation where children will feel, "I can't be the king, because he has blue eyes and I have brown eyes."

Tip:

Remember that you are building a play, not writing a story. If you create seven castles, you will eventually have to build them. If the tower you imagine is a hundred feet tall, you will have to explain why your platform is only four feet tall. It is perhaps better to just say the tower is "high." Let the group's imagination run wild, but keep practicality in your mind.

Enact:

Read the story aloud to the children. Evaluate the work you have done together on characters. Discuss:

★ Did we miss anything?

★ Is there anything new we heard this time through?

★ Do we want to change our minds about anyone?

Settings

Next work on settings. Explain:

★ I'm going to read the story again.

★ As I read, listen for information about places.

★ Where do things happen?

★ What is the weather like?

★ How do things look? Sound? Smell? Feel? *(Again, discourage discussion at this point. First you want them to listen again.)*

Then enact: read the story again. Define places in the same way you defined characters. If the entire story has a single setting, read the whole story through and then discuss the setting. If there are several locations, you may wish to stop and discuss each location as it appears.

Once again, make a list of descriptive words or a series of drawings.

Other good topics for discussing settings are:

★ time of day

★ day of the week

★ season

★ geographical location (as related to weather or culture)

★ descriptions of buildings, rooms, streets, etc.

Once you have created the list, read the story again, explaining first that you wish the group to imagine what these places are like. Begin by describing the first location and ask the group to close their eyes and imagine it. Continue reading, pausing at each new scene to describe the setting. Ask everyone to close their eyes and imagine it, then continue. Discuss afterward.

Tip:

It is helpful to designate a section of your work space for your lists or drawings, and leave them up throughout the process. That way everyone will be constantly reminded of the characters, the settings, etc., and you will have an atmosphere that shows your progress.

16

Action

The third element of building a play is *action*. What happens in the story? You may wish to start with an explanation of verbs. What are some things people do? (Run, sleep, go, eat, etc.) On the day you plan to work with actions, you can invite children to play Simon Says as a warm-up game. Use this game as an easy way to explain to young children what an action is. Invite them to show what they could do if "Simon says, 'eat'" or "Simon says, 'sleep.'"

Explain that this time they are to listen for the things that the characters are doing. Do stop frequently as you enact this reading. For each action, stop to define and discuss the action. You should end up with a list or a series of pictures that reads something like this:

★ Cinderella sweeps the floor.
★ Cinderella's stepsisters come into the room and see her.
★ Cinderella's stepsisters make fun of her.
★ Cinderella's stepsisters push her down.
★ Cinderella falls to the floor and cries.
★ Cinderella's stepsisters laugh and run out of the room.

Please note that these actions do not say things like "Cinderella's stepsisters are mean" or "Cinderella is unhappy." These are not actions. Actions are, well, *active*. When people act, they do things. These actions move the story forward.

Audiences do not understand what characters feel, only what the characters do or say. Audiences then interpret those actions and words. It is impossible to act the feeling of "cold." You cannot convey "cold" on stage. Try it. Are you rubbing your arms, blowing on your hands, pulling a blanket around yourself? What you are doing is "trying to get warm." You are showing how to *do* something, not how to *be* something.

Always choose action over feeling. As leader, you must be aware of the tendency to choose the latter, and correct it. When a child suggests "Cinderella's stepsisters are mean," respond with "Yes, they are. Now, what do those mean stepsisters *do?*"

When you have made your list, read through it from start to finish aloud. With the children, evaluate your work on actions:
★ Did we tell the whole story?
★ Does everything make sense?

You should be able to read the story and point to each action on the list. If you or the children are saying "But what about the part when...?"—you've missed something. Go back and add it in. When you have all the actions on your list, you're ready to create the play.

Getting Up Out of the Chairs

Now the children are ready to start "acting." You don't need to start handing out parts and running through the entire script right away. Start with the actions you've listed. How do you sweep a floor?

Everyone can do this at once. Ask the whole group to stand and pretend to sweep the floor. Use pantomime to create the various actions that will take place in the story. Children will have already experimented with simple pantomime in such focus games as Simon Says or Mirrors. Now they take those simple motions one step further.

Spend some time simply working on the actions of the story. When you're confident that the entire group understands the various actions, get the group spread out and read the story aloud. Ask the group to enact through pantomime the actions of the story as you read. Evaluate afterward: Which

actions worked best? Which parts of the story need more work? Your play is now beginning to take shape!

Adding Dialogue

When you have run through the pantomime version several times, and children are beginning to feel comfortable with the acted-out story, you're ready to move on to dialogue. You need not use only the author's words. You and your group can create dialogue together.

Explain that characters in the story not only do things, but also say things. (Dialogue, unlike action, *can* be based on feelings.) Now read the story (with the group seated) and stop whenever you come to a potential line of dialogue.

Sometimes this will be simple. The story will read:

"Cinderella swept the floor unhappily. 'Oh, what will I do?' she asked the mice."

The dialogue here is already written for you. The children can now take over this line from you. Learning this kind of lines isn't difficult—the children will probably already have the entire story memorized.

The new reading of this section will sound like this:

Leader: Cinderella swept the floor unhappily.

Children: Oh, what will I do?

Leader: she asked her mice friends.

Another way to find dialogue is to look for passages which read like this:

"Cinderella swept the floor unhappily. She asked her mice friends what she should do."

You must fill in that line of dialogue. Discuss it with your group. What would Cinderella say here? Agree on a line, and insert it. Feel free to change or delete parts of the narration at this point.

Leader: Cinderella swept the floor unhappily.

Children: What should I do?

Leader: she asked her mice friends.

The third situation you will encounter is when no dialogue exists at all. Perhaps you have a passage that reads as follows:

"Cinderella was very unhappy. She watched her stepsisters leave for the ball, knowing that she had a great deal of work to do while they were gone."

Tip: Strongly discourage screaming at this point. The players' instinct will be to shout every line. Don't let them get into that habit. Look back at the focus exercise on page 6 for a useful way to coach children on volume.

You may wish to add a "Goodbye, Cinderella" or a "Make sure to do the dishes, Cinderella" or a "Have a good time at the ball" to this section. Even if you decide in advance *where* to put the lines (a good idea), discuss the actual lines with the group. Let the players participate in the creative process by asking: "What would Cinderella say now?"

Read the story again, asking the group to say all lines. Repeat until you all feel comfortable with the "script" you have developed. Be sure you notate all lines in your working copy of the story! Improved dialogue is very easy to forget. If some or all of the children in the group can read, add the dialogue to your posted list of actions.

19

Putting it Together

Now comes the toughest day of the program: the day you put the words and the actions together. It's your patience and positive attitude that will make the difference in this session, so come prepared with both.

Tip:

Use a chart like the one on page 22 to schedule scenes with the same actors together. For example, Scene 1 uses Joe, John and Joyce and Scene 6 uses only Joe and John. If you schedule these for the same session, you will save unnecessary shuffling around of children. Notice also that Jill appears only in Scenes 3 and 4. Schedule these two together so that this actress doesn't need to come to two different sessions. You don't need to work the play in order.

Explain your plan to the children. Start by enacting the story as pantomime-only once, and as dialogue-only once to refresh everyone's memory.

Be prepared for chaos. Go slowly. Be patient. Enact the story with the pantomime and the lines together. Don't hesitate to stop and go back. Repeat until everyone feels comfortable.

Finally, evaluate. What worked? What didn't? Make any needed adjustments.

The Next Step

Your script is almost done. You've probably noticed that your story is beginning to look a great deal like a play! Of course, you still have everyone playing every part, and they are all standing in a group facing front, but what's left to do is not nearly as difficult as what you've already done.

It's time to give out parts. Now you will need to stress that each person is to say only his or her lines and perform his or her own actions! It may be helpful at this point to go back a step. Run through your story with the group seated so that the individual players can get used to their own lines. Then run the story with the lines and actions together.

Make no effort to place your performers on stage or change anything at this point. The actors will have enough to assimilate as it is! Get everyone up to speed in individual roles before you go any further.

What's Left?

You have a full script. You have a cast of characters who know their lines and know what to do. Now you need to tell them *where* to be. This is known as "blocking"—the process of placing the actors on the stage in relation to each other. (You'll find more information on blocking on page 32.)

You'll need to establish entrances and exits, and places to stand and sit. You'll need to work a bit on pacing. And finally, you'll need to add props, scenery and costumes. But first, figure out a workable rehearsal schedule.

How to Make a Play from a Script

You've chosen (or, together with the children, invented) a script. If you and the children have created the script together, you'll only need another four to six rehearsals before the performance. If you're just introducing the script, you'll need more time.

Either way, now you need to break the script down into workable chunks. Perhaps your script already has scene divisions, perhaps not. In any case, you will need to break it down still further.

Think back to the beginning of this book, when we discussed structuring your session. Figure out how much *actual rehearsal time* you will have in each session. For example, if you have one 45-minute session, and devote 5 minutes to warm-up, 10 minutes to games, 10 minutes to review and 5 minutes to general chaos, that leaves you *15 minutes* of actual rehearsal time.

Now figure out how many sessions you have left before the performance. You should plan for roughly 1/3 to 1/2 of these sessions to "stage" the play. You will use the rest for running scenes, dress rehearsals, review, etc. Say you have 20 sessions altogether. Figure on nine to do the initial work.

So you have nine 15-minute sessions to cover the script. First, break the script down into "French scenes" (scenes in which the beginning and ending are defined by the entrance or exit of any character). Go through the script and notate any time a character enters or exits. Now number these scenes sequentially.

This is just one possible breakdown, and it will not work for all scripts. In some shows all characters stay on all the time. In that case, find yourself another useful division, perhaps when characters first speak. In the script we provide, the play breaks naturally into ten scenes with a closing litany for eleven scenes altogether.

Tip:
Once you start the process of learning lines, memory becomes a big issue. Use the voice exercise explained on page 6 to aid memorization. Choose a troublesome line, and use it as the warm-up phrase. You can use a different line every day.

Make a chart to show who is on when:

Actor:	Scene: 1	2	3	4	5	6
Joe	x	x			x	x
John	x	x	x			x
Jane		x	x		x	
Joyce	x			x	x	
Jill			x	x		

A chart like the one above will be of inestimable value when planning a schedule. You have six scenes and nine sessions. Only you can decide how to use them. If the scenes are very short, perhaps you will want to work on three each session. If they are complicated, perhaps one per session. It's likely that you will have some combination of complex and simple scenes. Schedule accordingly. Now make yourself a schedule:

Session	Scene(s)	Actor(s)
1	1, 6	Joe, John, Joyce
2	2, 5	Joe, John, Jane, Joyce
3	3, 4	John, Jane, Jill, Joyce

Now you've covered all your scenes once. Notice that Joyce has been involved in every rehearsal so far. Perhaps she needs a session off:

Session	Scene(s)	Actor(s)
4	2, 3	Joe, John, Jane, Jill

Now give John a session off:

Session	Scene(s)	Actor(s)
5	4, 5	Joe, Jane, Joyce, Jill

22

What's left:

Session	Scene(s)	Actor(s)
6	1, 6	Joe, John, Joyce

Now you've scheduled every scene twice. Put the next three sessions on your calendar as "to be announced." You have no idea when you begin which scenes or which actors will need the most work. Leave yourself flexibility.

Sessions 7, 8 & 9: To be announced

As for the rest of the schedule, you have 11 sessions left.

Sessions 10 & 11: Work-through

These are sessions when you try to run the entire play with everyone—"putting it together" days. These sessions will be *disasters*. Plan on it. Don't be upset when it happens. You will not be able to do the whole play without stopping. You'll be lucky if you can get through one whole scene without stopping, and we suggest you not even try. These will be valuable rehearsals because you will be able to see easily where you need the most work.

Now think backwards from your last session to schedule the remaining work:

Sessions 18, 19, 20: full dress rehearsals (Three is a good number, but you could use one more or less, as you like.)

Session 17: emergency rehearsal (Always leave this day open to deal with, well, whatever you need to deal with. There's always one scene that really needs work.)

Session 16: runthrough without stopping (And without scripts! If you're still using scripts at this point, get rid of them *now!*)

This schedule leaves you Sessions 12-15 to turn the disaster of the first work-through into the joy of the first runthrough! Schedule them as needed.

Tip:
If in the middle of a session you find that everyone is fidgety, jump back to the warm-up. Do a short energy release, then a short focus activity to get them back on track.

Rehearsal Schedule – Session 1

Date: _____   Time: _____

Scene: _____   Scene: _____   Scene: _____

Characters:

_____	_____	_____
_____	_____	_____
_____	_____	
_____	_____	
_____	_____	
_____	_____	
_____	_____	
_____	_____	

Notes

Rehearsal Schedule – Session 2

Date: _____   Time: _____

Scene: _____   Scene: _____   Scene: _____

Characters:

_____	_____	_____
_____	_____	_____
_____	_____	_____
_____	_____	_____
_____	_____	_____
_____	_____	_____
_____	_____	_____
_____	_____	_____

Rehearsal Schedule – Session 3

Date: _____   Time: _____

Scene: _____   Scene: _____   Scene: _____

Characters:

_____   _____   _____

_____   _____   _____

_____   _____   _____

_____   _____   _____

_____   _____   _____

_____   _____   _____

_____   _____   _____

_____   _____   _____

_____   _____   _____

Notes

Rehearsal Schedule – Session 4

Date: _____   Time: _____

Scene: _____   Scene: _____   Scene: _____

Characters:

_____   _____   _____

_____   _____   _____

_____   _____   _____

_____   _____   _____

_____   _____   _____

_____   _____   _____

_____   _____   _____

_____   _____   _____

Rehearsal Schedule – Session 5

Date: _____   Time: _____

Scene: _____   Scene: _____   Scene: _____

Characters:

_____   _____   _____

_____   _____   _____

_____   _____   _____

_____   _____   _____

_____   _____   _____

_____   _____   _____

_____   _____   _____

Notes

Rehearsal Schedule – Session 6

Date: _____   Time: _____

Scene: _____   Scene: _____   Scene: _____

Characters:

_____   _____   _____

_____   _____   _____

_____   _____   _____

_____   _____   _____

_____   _____   _____

_____   _____   _____

_____   _____   _____

_____   _____   _____

Rehearsal Schedule – Session 7

Date: _____   Time: _____

Scene: _____   Scene: _____   Scene: _____

Characters:

_____	_____	_____
_____	_____	_____
_____	_____	_____
_____	_____	_____
_____	_____	_____
_____	_____	_____
_____	_____	_____
_____	_____	_____

Notes

Rehearsal Schedule – Session 8

Date: _____   Time: _____

Scene: _____   Scene: _____   Scene: _____

Characters:

_____	_____	_____
_____	_____	_____
_____	_____	_____
_____	_____	_____
_____	_____	_____
_____	_____	_____
_____	_____	_____
_____	_____	_____

Rehearsal Schedule – Session 9

Date: _____   Time: _____

Scene: _____   Scene: _____   Scene: _____

Characters:

_____   _____   _____

_____   _____   _____

_____   _____   _____

_____   _____

_____   _____

_____   _____

_____   _____

_____   _____

_____   _____

Notes

Rehearsal Schedule – Session 10

Date: _____   Time: _____

Scene: _____   Scene: _____   Scene: _____

Characters:

_____   _____   _____

_____   _____   _____

_____   _____   _____

_____   _____   _____

_____   _____   _____

_____   _____   _____

_____   _____   _____

_____   _____   _____

_____   _____   _____

Rehearsal Schedule – Session 11

Date: _____   Time: _____

Scene: _____   Scene: _____   Scene: _____

Characters:

_____   _____   _____

_____   _____   _____

_____   _____   _____

_____   _____   _____

_____   _____   _____

_____   _____   _____

_____   _____   _____

_____   _____   _____

Notes

Rehearsal Schedule – Session 12

Date: _____   Time: _____

Scene: _____   Scene: _____   Scene: _____

Characters:

_____   _____   _____

_____   _____   _____

_____   _____   _____

_____   _____   _____

_____   _____   _____

_____   _____   _____

_____   _____   _____

_____   _____   _____

Rehearsal Schedule – Session 13

Date: _____   Time: _____

Scene: _____   Scene: _____   Scene: _____

Characters:

_____   _____   _____

_____   _____   _____

_____   _____   _____

_____   _____   _____

_____   _____   _____

_____   _____   _____

_____   _____   _____

_____   _____   _____

Notes

Rehearsal Schedule – Session 14

Date: _____   Time: _____

Scene: _____   Scene: _____   Scene: _____

Characters:

_____   _____   _____

_____   _____   _____

_____   _____   _____

_____   _____   _____

_____   _____   _____

_____   _____   _____

_____   _____   _____

_____   _____   _____

Rehearsal Schedule – Session 15

Date: _____   Time: _____

Scene: _____   Scene: _____   Scene: _____

Characters:

_____   _____   _____

_____   _____   _____

_____   _____   _____

_____   _____   _____

_____   _____   _____

_____   _____   _____

_____   _____   _____

Notes

Rehearsal Schedule – Session 16

Date: _____   Time: _____

Scene: _____   Scene: _____   Scene: _____

Characters:

_____   _____   _____

_____   _____   _____

_____   _____   _____

_____   _____   _____

_____   _____   _____

_____   _____   _____

_____   _____   _____

Keep it Simple

In theatre, as in business, we have the "magic 3" of production values: good, cheap, quick. That's what we'd all like everything to be—good, cheap and quick.

Now remember that you can't ever have all three. Pick the two you want or need, and resign yourself to the fact that you'll never have the third. If you have a large budget, you can probably get it good and quick. If you have a very small budget, allow yourself plenty of time or you'll end up unhappy.

Remember that soliciting donations or dealing with volunteers takes time. Buying things takes money. If you have no time and no money, set your expectations *very* low, or you won't be happy with the result.

Simple Settings

Settings don't have to be complicated or expensive. The most important functions stages and sets serve are to define the playing area and to provide places for the actors to sit, stand and lean. The functions of indicating "where" the action takes place and establishing the mood of the play are secondary.

Defining the playing area can be as simple as taping off a square on the floor, or putting chairs for spectators in a circle. Use whatever works for your space.

The traditional stage is known as the "proscenium" stage. This is the arrangement where the audience sits on only one side of the stage. Broadway theaters, movie theaters and school plays are most often set up this way.

Even if you think your group is too young to understand, you should know how to interpret simple stage directions. All stage directions are given from the actors' point of view. In other words, the term "stage right" means "to the actors' right, if they are facing the audience."

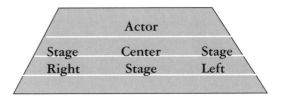

The terms used for moving toward and away from the audience are "downstage" and "upstage." Upstage means toward the back, or away from the audience. Downstage means toward the front, or closer to the audience.

There are nine basic places to stand on a proscenium or thrust stage:

UR (upstage right)	UC (upstage center)	UL (upstage left)
RC (right center)	C (center)	LC (left center)
DR (downstage right)	DC (downstage center)	DL (downstage left)

Audience

These are extremely helpful notations for yourself when you want to remember where everyone goes. Get used to using them, and make notes in your script. Force yourself to say "walk down" instead of "walk forward" and you'll all get accustomed to these useful terms.

Once you have defined a "playing space," you may wish to create "wings"—places where the actors can enter and exit without being seen—to the left and right of the stage. The left and right wings are referred to as "off-stage right" and "offstage left." You may also need a "crossover" (a place where the actors can cross from stage right to stage left without being seen) all the way upstage.

Typically some sort of material blocks the audience's vision of the crossover area. This material, known commonly as "masking," is most often made from curtains or "flats" (fake walls made from wood, fabric with a wood frame, or cardboard).

Simple Scenery and Props

Once you have "built" your stage, put whatever you want on it. The most important thing is to mind the "sightlines." That is, make sure the audience can see everything. Don't put a tall bookshelf downstage of a table.

Tip:

If you want to make it easier for the actors to know where to stand, take a tip from the dancers of the world: run a piece of masking tape along the front of the playing area, and label it with numbers, colors or pictures. Do this before the first rehearsal. The children can then learn that they are to stand at number 4, or in the blue section, and retain that positioning when you move to your actual stage.

Tip:

When you set up your stage, go into the audience seating area and walk through every aisle and in front of every seat. There will be things you can see from one seat and not another. Sit in random seats, to the left, the right, the front, the back. Don't just sit in the middle and assume the whole audience will be able to see everything.

Backdrops

This is fancier than most groups will want for a simple play for parents, but if you live in a large city, painted backdrops are an easy way to indicate a locale. Many are available to rent on a weekly basis, and come in various sizes and designs. There exist hundreds of different indoor and outdoor scenes, as well as more abstract designs. These backdrops usually come equipped with ties on top for attaching to a pipe.

Cardboard, for either scenery or props, is relatively inexpensive, lightweight, and takes paint beautifully. Painted panels make great set pieces!

Props

Mostly you'll get these in the time-honored way: sending notes home with the children asking their parents to loan needed props to the show. If you're looking for furniture, try the local stores in town, especially used furniture stores. Often places will loan pieces to non-profit organizations in exchange for an ad in the program, or a sign saying "Furniture from Joe's Furniture Outlet." This is a good deal all around. Just be careful about damage.

A word about safety: Every piece of wood, cloth and cardboard you put on stage, as well as any paint you use, should be fireproofed. Don't take chances! You don't need to buy expensive already-fireproofed materials. You can buy liquid fireproofing and paint it on everything yourself.

Simple Publicity and Programs

Most often, a simple play will be performed only for the school and the children's parents. If you *do* want a larger audience, you will need publicity. So how can you fill those seats?

Make up a batch of flyers and send them home with the kids! Your best audience is going to come primarily from the family, friends, neighbors and acquaintances of your performers. Make it easy for them. Copy a single page flyer on colored paper, and let the performers each take a bunch home.

Flyers

Vital information for a flyer:

★ name of show
★ day and date of show
★ curtain time
★ location of show
★ contact phone number
★ ticket price (if any)

Desirable information for a flyer:

★ short description of the show (i.e. "A medieval Christmas pageant performed by the St. Matthew's Youth Group")
★ time the doors will open
★ directions or simple map to the performance space
★ "box office" hours

Tip:
If you're looking for tips for set arrangements, watch TV sitcoms. These are taped in front of live audiences, and their furniture is arranged for the stage.

Always try to include artwork on your flyer —it makes people look.

Flyers can also be placed in store windows and on counters of any local business. Just be sure to ask the staff's permission first. Don't forget neighborhood restaurants, hospitals, hotels and laundromats. The more bored the patrons are, the more likely it is they will read your flyer. Think, too, about places where parents are likely to take their kids— parks, doctors' offices, fast food burger stands and children's clothing stores.

Offer to swap flyers with other non-profit organizations like yours: churches, youth centers or schools. Look for community service bulletin boards at the library, the police station, the fire department, the supermarket or at local government offices.

Never forget that your best bets are found in internal resources: your own congregation, other classes in your school, the teachers' lounge or the PTA. Conversely, distributing flyers randomly in mailboxes or on cars is time consuming and sometimes against local ordinances. We'd advise you to skip that idea.

Another kind of publicity to try: the local papers often have listings of events for no charge. Be aware that their deadlines are frequently much earlier than you think they are. Contact all the newspapers in your area as soon as you have your dates, and find out when these deadlines are so you don't miss them.

Call the local radio station—high school and college radio stations are terrific for this—and ask if they will read or record a public service announcement for you.

Programs

Programs can be as simple as flyers. Vital information for programs include:

★ names of all performers and staff (Include everyone who worked on the project, on-stage and off—the people who built the set, the people who stuck flyers up in every laundry in town and the people who set up chairs.)

★ a brief description of your organization and its goals, and a note from the organizer of the program

★ a "special thanks" section—thank people who have loaned you materials, the parent who drove the car pool, the teacher who watched your class for 5 minutes every time you had to run out to deal with a problem, the diner that gave out 500 flyers. People who are appreciated are more likely to help you again.

If you have an intermission, state that. If you have fire ordinances, list them. If you're selling refreshments, say that too. Most importantly, use your program to promote your next event(s). The people in the audience actually showed up, and might again! If you have no next event in the near future, promote another group's event. Again, help them, and they'll help you.

Simple Organizing Devices: Plots and Prop Table

A "plot" is basically a list or a chart, which describes everything about one particular aspect of your play. For example, you will need a prop plot. "Props" (short for "properties") are things that the actors use which are not attached to the set or the costumes. Books, dishes, letters and brooms are all props.

Your prop plot should have the following sections:

★ item
★ character (who uses it first)
★ page (it first appears on)
★ preset (where the item should be at the beginning of the play)
★ end (where the item should be at the end of the play)
★ notes

You can also make a section on this plot entitled "From" to keep track of where you will get the item (buy, rent, make, borrow). If you have a long, complicated list, you may want a separate page for the "From" information, so you can keep track of budget, materials, lenders (to return and to thank), etc.

The best way to make a plot is to get some colored pencils and start circling things in your script. Choose a color for each element, such as red for props, blue for costumes, green for sound effects, etc. Read the script and circle all props in red. Don't forget to read and circle stage directions, since they will contain prop information too.

Draw a line from your circle out to the margin, and write the name of the item on the line:

NARRATOR ONE:	In the beginning, God made heaven and earth. God called it good. And God made a man and a woman to be friends.
EVE:	God's garden is so beautiful, Adam. *(She kneels to smell a beautiful flower.)* — flower
ADAM:	And filled with good things for us. *(He reaches for a fruit and eats it.)* — fruit
EVE:	*(She stands and looks at an imaginary or prop/painted tree.)* And sometimes—I think that tree is the most beautiful tree of all.

Now you have a clear list on each page from which to make your plot. It's very easy to circle something and then miss it. You will want to go through the script several times for each element, and then be prepared to discover that you have missed things even still.

Prop Plot

Scene	Page	Item	Used by	Preset	Ends	Notes

Keeping track of props is notoriously difficult. They disappear easily under chairs, in pockets, in the dressing room, and behind the curtains. Set a big prop table at each side of the stage, and cover it with securely taped brown paper. Then take a big black marker and trace the outline of each prop, and write its name within the outline. You will see immediately when something is missing.

Do this as soon as you have even one prop. Emphasize that all props *must* be returned to their proper places each and every time they are used. Discourage children from touching a prop except for its intended use.

Come to Bethlehem
Production Notes

Come to Bethlehem is a simple "play from scratch" Christmas pageant, suitable for use with 4- to 8-year-olds. (See page 11 for more information on "How to Make a Play from Scratch.")

The play is built on the familiar Christmas carol, "O Come, All Ye Faithful." After an opening chorus of the carol, children play the parts of different characters coming to Bethlehem, all looking for something—and all led to the manger where baby Jesus lies. The play concludes with another chorus of the carol.

This play is especially useful for those who wish to make a simple, appealing Christmas play with young children. The children will enjoy inventing their own characters and lines, and grownups can enjoy their children's imagination elaborating the details of a simple, straightforward plot. Allow plenty of time for children to develop the play together, and don't be discouraged if show time surprises you with performances quite different from those careful practices. Everyone will still enjoy themselves, as long as you do!

The focal point of the production will be a small manger with a baby Jesus. A large baby-sized basket can work, as could a wooden crate filled with hay or blankets. A baby doll wrapped in a plain baby blanket can serve as baby Jesus.

If possible, print the lyrics to "O Come, All Ye Faithful" on a program for the audience. Include the first and sixth verses and refrain.

Children can improvise simple costumes. Biblical characters, such as shepherds, can be dressed in costumes made from lengths of cloth belted with ropes or scarves. (See pages 47 and 49.) Contemporary characters, if they appear, will need different costumes—a badge for a police officer, or a giant pizza box for a delivery person.

Cast of Characters

Gatekeeper: This character serves as both a narrator and stage manager. You might play this part yourself, or ask for the help of an adult or older—fifth grade and up—child.

All other characters will be determined by the children themselves, with your help. After the children have made those decisions, list those characters and their players on the cast grid provided on page 42.

O come, all ye faithful,
Joyful and triumphant,
O come ye, O come ye
To Bethlehem.
Come, and behold him,
Born the king of angels:
O come, let us adore him,
O come, let us adore him,
O come, let us adore him,
Christ the Lord.

Yea, Lord, we greet thee,
Born this happy morning,
Jesus, to thee be
Glory given.
Word of the Father,
Now in flesh appearing:
O come, let us adore him,
O come, let us adore him,
O come, let us adore him,
Christ the Lord.

Scripts: Three Christmas Plays

Cast Grid

Name	Phone	Character	Permission slip	Costume measured	Script given	Script returned

Developing the Play

This kind of play does not have a set script, or even a cast of characters. Instead you and the children will develop the play together, following the basic process presented in "How to Make a Play from Scratch," pages 11-13.

The opening situation is baby Jesus sleeping in Bethlehem. Especially for younger children, present the situation by presenting its focal point: a baby in a manger in Bethlehem.

Gather the children around the baby. Invite them to talk about who the baby is. Who is Jesus? What is Bethlehem? As necessary, help them understand that Bethlehem is the name of a place, the place where Jesus was born. Many, many people traveled to Bethlehem when Jesus was born.

Invite children to imagine that they are traveling to Bethlehem, where baby Jesus sleeps. Ask them:

★ Who are you?
★ Where did you come from?
★ Why are you here?

In the play, these same questions can be asked by the gatekeeper. This makes an easy cue for the children to help them remember the dialogue they invent. When we tried this idea with several kindergartners and first graders, we got enough imaginative answers to make an enjoyable play. Who are you?

★ I'm a goat! Me-aa-aa...
★ I'm a queen.
★ We're shepherds. (Two inseparable buddies chose this.)
★ We're swimmers!

Any of these answers would serve as a character for either one brave child alone to enact, or several children together. You'll be amazed at how quickly young children fall into character. The queen said all her words in serene, regal tones. The goat was an appealing comic, and the swimmer a determined overachiever.

The next question was: Where did you come from?

★ Me-aa-aa... (accompanied by expressive goat shoulder-shrugs)
★ I came from Denver.
★ We came from a cave.
★ We swam from the ocean to get here.

The last question was: Why are you here?

★ Me-aa-aa...(urgent head nods in the direction of the rest of the stage)
★ I'm looking for baby Jesus.
★ We're looking for our lost sheep.
★ To find Jesus.

In enacting the play, the gatekeeper asked each child or group of children all three questions, one at a time, when the character approached the gate. After the goat had

43

given her answers, she wandered around the stage, making soft goat noises and nuzzling aside furniture to look for baby Jesus. The queen, shepherds and swimmers spoke their pieces in succession, then joined in the search, each keeping in character. (The queen would raise a regally distressed hand to her cheek at each failure to find baby Jesus.)

To bring the play to a resolution, we asked: Who could show them where baby Jesus is? The children unanimously chose Mary, and gave her the dialogue, "Hey, everybody! He's right here!"

Each child or group of children then came and spoke to the baby Jesus to bring the play to its conclusion. The goat gave another long bleat, while nuzzling the baby with her beard. The queen picked up the baby and gave it a loud, smacking kiss. The swimmers offered the baby some milk. And one shepherd got a genuine laugh, when, hand on one hip, he gave the baby a serious look and asked, "Excuse me, but have you seen our sheep?"

Finish this simple play with the audience singing the chorus of "O Come, All Ye Faithful."

Many Miles to Bethlehem
Production Notes

Many Miles to Bethlehem is a Christmas pageant based on a story in print. We provide the text for this story, but you can also purchase *Many Miles to Bethlehem*, an oversized picture book with this story (and two other stories for Advent and Christmas) from Spindle Press (1-800-824-1813). This play uses the methods described in "How to Make a Play from a Story." (See page 14.) You can use those methods with *any* published Christmas story suitable for 4- to 10-year-olds. We recommend that you choose one based on original text, rather than one that uses the unadorned Nativity story from Luke 2:1-11.

The play moves from opening situation, to a series of obstacles, to the final "happy ending": the birth of baby Jesus. Help the children see that the problem for Mary and Joseph was finding a safe place where Jesus could be born. You might want to build the opening situation into a more dramatic opening by including the background information that is only implied in the story as written:

★ Mary is pregnant. It's almost time for her baby to be born. She has worked hard to make her home ready for her new baby.

★ Joseph hears bad news: by order of the country's ruler, he and Mary cannot stay at home, but must travel to far-off Bethlehem.

Many Miles to Bethlehem tells the rest of the story: how Mary and Joseph make the hard trip to Bethlehem, only to find no room for them at all, until an innkeeper lets them have one part of a stable where they can stay.

Now use the information in "How to Make a Play from a Story" (pages 14-20) to make the story into a play, beginning with the first step: reading the story to the children.

Story: Many Miles to Bethlehem

Mary wraps bread in a clean cloth. Joseph ties jars of water to the donkey's back.

"Don't forget these," Mary says. Clean cloths to cuddle a newborn baby.

Time to leave for Bethlehem.

Miles to go, the way so slow,
So many miles to Bethlehem.

Joseph and Mary walk for days. By night the air grows cold, and it is hard to sleep. By day the sun blazes, and it is hard to walk.

They walk on roads made of dirt and sand. The donkey's legs are brown with dust.

Hoof steps sound, on the stony ground,
All the miles to Bethlehem.

Does all the world walk with us? The roads are filled with people traveling back to the towns where they were born.

Mary's back aches, but she rubs her hands on her belly and keeps walking. Joseph's feet ache, but he leads the donkey steadily on.

Still we walk, too tired to talk.
How many miles to Bethlehem?

In Bethlehem, the streets and houses overflow with families. Mary and Joseph walk from house to inn, but there is no room for them anywhere.

"You can stay in the stable with my animals," says one innkeeper. She leads them to a rough cave behind the inn.

A bare dirt floor, and nothing more,
After all those miles to Bethlehem.

That very night, in that very stable, Mary gives birth to a baby
boy, her first child. She wraps him in the clean cloths.

Mary holds her baby close, as she leans against the warm fur of the
gentle donkey. Joseph looks into the night and whispers, "Thank
you, God, for baby Jesus."

The stars rise, a baby cries,
This holy night in Bethlehem.

Production Notes (continued)

If you include the rhymed verses in the final script of the play, they could be chanted by a group of children who form the "chorus" of the play, or by several individual children taking turns. Three settings are implied in the story as written: Mary and Joseph's house, the road to Bethlehem and the stable in Bethlehem.

Many of the children will have heard the Christmas story before. Encourage them to imagine themselves into the story where they can improvise freely dialogue and actions. Do not be concerned with sticking too closely to the framework given in *Many Miles to Bethlehem*.

Since the characters will all be characters from a biblical time, help the children make simple costumes. (See the illustration on the facing page.)

List the characters and their players on the cast grid provided on page 50.

Cast of Characters

The children will determine the exact list, but possibilities include:

Mary

Joseph

donkey

travelers to Bethlehem

innkeepers

Cast Grid

Name	Phone	Character	Permission slip	Costume measured	Script given	Script returned

The Jesse Tree
Production Notes

The Jesse Tree is a more elaborate Advent or Christmas pageant based on a full script, especially suitable for use with 7- to 10-year-olds. The play consists of ten short vignettes tied together with the visual prop of a large Jesse tree. (The Jesse Tree is an Advent devotion based on Old Testament symbols and stories about God's promised Messiah. We've adapted this popular custom to make an offbeat play.)

After each vignette, one or more symbols are placed on the tree, as the narrator recites lines tying the symbol or symbols to the coming of Jesus Christ. The play concludes with a short litany based on the symbol-filled tree.

This format is easily adapted by religious day schools (or after-school care programs) who can make time to work with the children involved in each vignette during free play periods. If you are pulling together the pageant for a Sunday religious education program, get started early, and expect to schedule extra rehearsals as the play dates approach.

The focal point of the production will be the Jesse tree (which should be large and entirely visible to the audience) and its symbols. You can use an actual Christmas tree for the Jesse tree, or construct a large felt banner on which symbols can be taped or pinned as the play progresses. Symbols should be prepared ahead of time. We recommend inviting children to work together to construct colorful collage designs on circles cut from poster board. Make the symbols large—at least 15" in diameter.

You will need the following symbols:

Scene one	Adam and Eve
	apple
Scene two	Noah and his wife
	rainbow
Scene three	Abraham and Sarah
	stars
Scene four	Moses, Aaron and Miriam
	tambourine
Scene five	Joshua
	grapes
Scene six	David, Solomon, Ruth, Naomi
	crown
Scene seven	Ezekiel
	scrolls
Scene eight	Mary
	rose
Scene nine	Joseph
	carpenter's tools
Scene ten	Jesus
	manger

52

Keep costumes simple. Children will switch roles frequently. You can get an inexpensive but unified look by asking each child to dress in blue jeans and a solid-color tee shirt in Advent colors: purple, blue or rose. Add the *simplest* details to help each child make the transition to another part: a veil fashioned from a scarf for Mary, for example, or a broomstick staff for Noah. When children play animals, they can don a set of ears, a tail or a paper mask for the quickest possible transition.

Each scene follows the same format:
★ *Narrator One* sets the scene with a quick background narration.
★ Children act out the scene.
★ *Narrator Two* reads aloud a Bible verse connected with the symbol for that scene, as a child carries the symbol across the stage to the Jesse tree.

List the characters and their players on the cast grid provided on page 54.

Cast of Characters

(Because each vignette stands alone, you can re-use actors again and again. This play will work well with either a small or large group of children.)

Narrator One (adult or youth reader)
Narrator Two (adult or youth reader)

Adam	Moses
Eve	Miriam
	Aaron
Noah	Hebrews
Noah's children	
	Joshua
Abraham	Rahab
three angels	Naomi
Sarah	Ruth
Joseph	
Joseph's family	Samuel
	David
Elijah	Solomon
Elisha	
Isaiah	Ezra
Jeremiah	Nehemiah
Mary	
Joseph	

Tip:
To make the sound of thunder, use a sheet of aluminum. Hang or lay it on a table and flex the sheet of metal back and forth to hear realistic thunder!

Cast Grid

Name	Phone	Character(s)	Permission slip	Costume measured	Script given	Script returned	

Script: The Jesse Tree
Scene One: Adam and Eve

(The play opens on a Christmas tree or empty Jesse tree banner to the back and center—upstage center—of the performance area.)

NARRATOR ONE:	In the beginning, God made heaven and earth. God called it good. And God made a man and a woman to be friends.
EVE:	God's garden is so beautiful, Adam. *(She kneels to smell a beautiful flower.)*
ADAM:	And filled with good things for us. *(He reaches for a fruit and eats it.)*
EVE:	*(She stands and looks at an imaginary or prop/painted tree.)* And sometimes—I think that tree is the most beautiful tree of all.
ADAM:	We can't go near it, Eve! God said not to eat from it!
EVE:	Not to eat from it, no. But how could it hurt just to go close? *(She walks slowly to the tree, her eyes fixed on its fruit.)*
ADAM:	*(He follows Eve to the tree.)* It is...the most beautiful fruit I've ever seen.
EVE:	*(She reaches her hand to touch the fruit.)* Yes. And I have heard that if we DID eat this fruit, we would become like God.
ADAM:	Just like God?
EVE:	Yes...*(She closes her hand around the fruit and picks it. She lifts it to her mouth and takes a bite. The bite is delicious and she offers the fruit to Adam, who also takes a bite. For one moment, they enjoy the*

fruit in silence. Then a great clap of thunder comes, and they drop the fruit in fear. They join hands and run.)

NARRATOR TWO: Blessed is the fruit of your womb: Jesus. *(As the narrator recites this verse, the apple symbol is placed on the Jesse tree.)*

Scene Two: Ark and Rainbow

NARRATOR ONE: People did not stay in God's beautiful garden. They fought with one another and even killed. One day God told Noah to build an ark to save people and animals from the rains that would come and wash the earth.

NOAH: Hurry! The rain will start soon!

CHILD: There are only a few animals more. *(Animals come two by two into the an ark. Use a table draped with cloth or a cardboard appliance box with an opening at the back as the base of the ark.)*

CROWD: Silly man! Look at that stupid boat! Crazy old Noah! *(Assign these and similar phrases to different children to create a realistic crowd sound.)*

NOAH'S WIFE: Oh! The first drops! Come, children. *(She takes two children into the ark.)*

NOAH: *(He helps the last animals inside, then turns to the crowd and says simply:)* Goodbye.

NARRATOR ONE: Rain fell for forty days. The ark sailed for even more days, while all those inside the ark waited for the waters to go down.

NOAH'S WIFE: Come out! It's safe now! Come! *(She leads out one of the animals, followed by Noah and a child, each leading another animal.)*

CHILD: Father, what if it happens again?

NOAH: It will never happen again. God has promised us. And look!

NARRATOR TWO: Whenever I cover the sky with clouds and the rainbow appears, I will remember my promise to you and to all. *(Genesis 9:14-15a,* Today's English Version. *As the narrator recites this verse, the rainbow symbol is placed on the Jesse tree.)*

Scene Three: Abraham and Sarah

NARRATOR ONE: But Noah's children and their children did not always remember God's love for them. Again people went their own ways, and lived without paying attention to God. But God would never give up.

ABRAHAM: Sarah! I must talk to you.

SARAH: What is it, Abraham?

ABRAHAM: We must leave our home, Sarah. God has said so.

SARAH: But all our family lives here! Our mothers, fathers, brothers, sisters. How can we leave them all?

ABRAHAM: It will be hard. But God loves us even more. Can we say no?

SARAH: Abraham, where will we live?

ABRAHAM: I don't know yet. God will bring us to our new home.

SARAH: Leave the home we know. Say goodbye to our family. Oh, Abraham. What will we have left?

ABRAHAM: We will have each other, Sarah. And God. And children! God has promised us many, many children.

SARAH: We're too old for children!

ABRAHAM: Not if God sends them. Please, Sarah. Come with me? (*He reaches out his hand.*)

SARAH: (*Slowly she walks to him and takes his hand.*) Yes, Abraham. (*She looks away, to the road ahead and says, in the same exact voice:*) Yes, God.

NARRATOR TWO: Look at the sky and try to count the stars; you will have as many descendants as that. (*Genesis 15:5b,* Today's English Version. *As the narrator recites this verse, the stars symbol is placed on the Jesse tree.*)

Scene Four: Leaving Egypt

NARRATOR ONE: God did send children to Abraham and Sarah. Those children had children of their own, and the children of Abraham were as many as the stars in the sky. But even the lives of these people of God were not always easy. Hard times came, and God's people became slaves in the land of Egypt. Even in Egypt, God remembered them.

MOSES: Come! This is the night. You will leave the land of Egypt and never be slaves again.

HEBREW ONE: But, Moses, the Egyptians will catch us and bring us back!

HEBREW TWO: Or even kill us!

AARON: No! Have faith in God. God will never let us down.

HEBREW THREE: And then what will we do, Aaron? We'll starve in the desert.

MIRIAM:	God feeds every bird in the sky, every horse in the field, every fish in the sea. God will feed God's own people.
MOSES:	Listen to Miriam. We must go NOW! *(They begin to make their way. They come to a "river" of blue cloths.)*
HEBREW ONE:	Look! The Egyptians are close behind!
HEBREW TWO:	And the river is too deep for us to cross!
HEBREW THREE:	We'll never get away now.
MIRIAM:	Don't give up!
MOSES:	The Egyptians will never take us back. *(He stretches his arm out over the water, and two children pull the cloths apart. The people walk across, cheering. Aaron, Miriam and Moses go last. On the other side, Miriam brings out a tambourine.)*
MIRIAM:	We're saved! Let us dance.
AARON AND MOSES:	Praise God!
HEBREWS:	Yes, praise God! *(The people clap, cheer and dance.)*
NARRATOR TWO:	The prophet Miriam took her tambourine, and sang for them: Sing to the Lord, because he has won a glorious victory. *(Exodus 15:20-21,* Today's English Version. *As the narrator recites this verse, the tambourine symbol is placed on the Jesse tree.)*

Scene Five: The New Land

NARRATOR ONE:	Moses led God's people back to the land of Abraham and Sarah. He chose spies to go and see what the land was like.

HEBREW ONE: Look, the spies Moses sent are coming back.

HEBREW TWO: What did you find?

JOSHUA: Listen! The land is good, and we will be happy there. Plenty of food grows there: grain and olives and grapes. *(Shows basket of food.)*

HEBREW ONE: Yes! God has brought us to a good place.

SPY ONE: Wait! Yes, good food grows there. But so do giants! The land is full of them!

SPY TWO: We'll never be able to live there. The giants will chase us out.

HEBREW TWO: Giants? What should we do?

HEBREW ONE: We must turn back at once.

JOSHUA: No, don't be afraid! God has brought us here. God will take care of us in our new home.

HEBREW TWO: But we can't fight giants!

JOSHUA: God will fight for you!

HEBREWS AND SPIES: No! We won't go!

JOSHUA: No? Then we will go back to the desert. Some day I will bring your children to this land, but not one of you will ever taste its good food.

NARRATOR TWO: Taste and see that God is good. Happy are those who trust in God. *(Psalm 34:8, paraphrased. As the narrator recites this verse, the grapes symbol is placed on the Jesse tree.)*

60

Scene Six: Family Stories

DAVID: *(He is seated on a bench. He gives a small scroll to the messenger standing by.)* Go and take this message to the general.

HEBREW ONE: Yes, King David.

SOLOMON: Father! Father!

HEBREW TWO: Your father is busy, Solomon.

DAVID: But not too busy for you, Solomon. Come here. *(He pats the bench next to him. Solomon runs to him and sits down.)* Now what do you want from your father this morning?

SOLOMON: I want a story!

DAVID: *(He laughs.)* Always a story! And which story do you want to hear?

SOLOMON: The story of your great-grandmother Ruth, please.

DAVID: Ah...she was a brave and loving woman, my great-grandmother, who came from so far away. And so was my great-great-grandmother Naomi, who went to live with her sons in a far-away land. *(Scene shifts to the women about whom David tells his story.)*

NAOMI: Ruth. Orpah. Come walk with me.

RUTH AND
  ORPAH: Yes, Naomi.

NAOMI: So many sad days this year. When Mahlon and Chillon died, who was more sad? I lost my sons, but you lost your husbands.

61

RUTH:	I thought our tears would never stop.
NAOMI:	And this will be another sad day. I must return home and leave you, dear Orpah and Ruth.
ORPAH:	No, Naomi! Don't leave us! Come back with us to our country!
NAOMI:	I want to go back to my home. But you, my daughters, go back to your homes with God's blessing and mine. *(Orpah hugs Naomi, and leaves, waving goodbye.)* Ruth? Will you let me bless you, too?
RUTH:	No, Naomi. And I will not let you leave me, either!
NAOMI:	Ruth, I want to go home to the land of Abraham and Sarah and my God.
RUTH:	Then I will go, too. Don't tell me to go away, Naomi! Your God will be my God. Your people will be my people. Please, Naomi.
NAOMI:	Oh, Ruth. My dearest daughter. *(They embrace.)*
RUTH:	Now. Let us go to your home together. *(Scene returns to David and Solomon.)*
SOLOMON:	And did they live here forever, Father?
DAVID:	Yes, Solomon. And Ruth was the mother of Obed, who was the father of Jesse.
SOLOMON:	And Jesse was the father of YOU, king of all God's people.
DAVID:	And I am the father of YOU! And it is time for YOU to run to your lessons. Learn them well, Solomon, because some day you, too, will be king and must know how to serve God's people.

NARRATOR TWO: I will make him my first-born son, the greatest of all kings. I will always keep my promise to him. (*Psalm 89:27-28a,* Today's English Version. *As the narrator recites this verse, the crown symbol is placed on the Jesse tree.*)

Scene Seven: From Far Away

NARRATOR ONE: Not all the kings of Israel followed God. In those days, God's people knew the hardest times of all. The rich did not share with the poor. The people did not listen to God's word. God's people lost great wars, and were taken away to strange countries. But even in those far-away places, God sent prophets to tell God's word.

HEBREW ONE: Can God have forgotten us?

HEBREW TWO: I do not know. We are gone from our homes. We work long hours for our masters.

HEBREW THREE: I wonder if we will ever return home.

HEBREW ONE: Look. There's Ezekiel.

HEBREW TWO: Ezekiel, has God forgotten us?

EZEKIEL: No, God remembers us. Listen to these words from God. (*He unrolls a scroll.*) God says, "I will be like a good shepherd to my people, who are like lost sheep. I will take care of them. I will bring them home." (*He walks off as the Hebrews work again.*)

MESSENGER: Israelites! A message from Cyrus the king: Go back to Jerusalem. Build there a temple for your God.

HEBREW THREE: Home? We're going home!

HEBREW ONE: Run and tell everyone! We're going HOME! (*All the people drop their work tools and dance, cheer, etc.*)

NARRATOR TWO: Lord, you have the words that give eternal life. (*John 6:68, Today's English Version. As the narrator recites this verse, the scroll symbol is placed on the Jesse tree.*)

Scene Eight: Mary

NARRATOR ONE: And so God's people returned home. But still they waited for another king, like good King David, who would lead God's people. Still prophets came to promise this king who would live forever. Years and tens of years and hundreds of years passed. And all Israel waited.

(*Mary hums a tune as she works at cleaning, weaving or a similar task. Her back is turned to the angel who walks onto the stage, but stays at a distance.*)

ANGEL: Mary, I greet you.

(*Mary turns and drops her broom, spindle, etc. She gasps at the sight of the angel.*)

ANGEL: Mary, don't be afraid. God is with you. God has chosen you, Mary, to be the mother of a special child. He will be king of all God's people.

MARY: Me? But how can I? I haven't even married Joseph yet!

ANGEL: This will be God's own child, and you will be his mother. You must call him Jesus.

MARY:	I will do what God wants. I will be the mother of Jesus. (*The angel bows to her and leaves.*) I must go tell Joseph! (*She runs off.*)
NARRATOR TWO:	The desert will rejoice, and flowers will bloom in the waste-lands. (*Isaiah 35:1,* Today's English Version. *As the narrator recites this verse, the rose symbol is placed on the Jesse tree.*)

Scene Nine: Joseph

NARRATOR ONE:	A child is coming! But God wants someone to help Mary care for the baby who will be king. (*A line divides the stage in half. On one side is Joseph's "house": a sleeping pallet, his work tools and a few dishes. On the other side is Mary's "house." Mary runs to the line dividing the two houses. They can talk as if they are outside, face to face, or as if they are talking through adjoining windows or over a fence.*)
MARY:	Joseph! I have amazing news!
JOSEPH:	What news, Mary?
MARY:	I'm going to have a baby!
JOSEPH:	A baby? Mary, you're not supposed to have a baby. We're not married yet.
MARY:	But this will be God's baby, Joseph! An angel told me!
JOSEPH:	An angel told you? Mary—I don't understand this. I don't like this. And I don't think I want to marry you anymore.

(He turns away. Mary looks after him sadly, then goes to her bed and lies down. Joseph gets ready for bed, then lies down. Their backs are turned to each other. An angel enters Joseph's house.)

ANGEL: Joseph! I am God's angel. Don't be afraid. Make Mary your wife. All she tells you is true.

(The angel leaves. Joseph wakes and looks, but the angel is gone.)

JOSEPH: Was it real? Was it a dream? What should I do? *(He paces the floor, then stops.)* I don't know the answers, but I do know Mary. *(He runs to Mary's house.)* Mary! Wake up, please?

MARY: *(She comes to him.)* What is it, Joseph?

JOSEPH: Mary, I'm sorry. Will you still marry me?

MARY: Oh, yes, Joseph! *(They leave together.)*

NARRATOR TWO: The stone which the builders rejected turned out to be the most important of all. *(Psalm 118:22,* Today's English Version. *As the narrator recites this verse, the carpenter's tools symbol is placed on the Jesse tree.)*

Scene Ten: Go to Bethlehem!

NARRATOR ONE: And so Joseph brought Mary to Bethlehem in time for Jesus to be born. They slept in a stable of animals, because no one could find them a house or even a room. Only the animals heard the baby's first cry. But in a field far away, shepherds watched their sheep.

SHEPHERD ONE: I'm so tired tonight. I think I shall sleep until noon!

SHEPHERD TWO: And my feet are so sore running after the sheep all day!

SHEPHERD THREE:	At least now we can rest for a while.
SHEPHERD ONE:	What's that light? Who is it? What is it?
ANGEL:	Don't be afraid! I have great news for you! Go to Bethlehem, you who are the poorest of God's people. You'll find a treasure just for you: a baby who will be your king, and who will live forever.
ANGELS:	Glory to God! And peace to God's people! *(The angels disappear.)*
SHEPHERD TWO:	Come on! Let's go see this baby!
SHEPHERD THREE:	What about those sore feet of yours?
SHEPHERD TWO:	Who cares! Let's go!
NARRATOR TWO:	You will find a baby wrapped in cloths and lying in a manger. *(Luke 2:12,* Today's English Version. *As the narrator recites this verse, the manger symbol is placed on the Jesse tree.)*
CLOSING LITANY:	Come, Lord Jesus
	(Children gather around the finished Jesse tree. They take turns leading this litany, touching or holding up each symbol named in turn. All the children join in the refrain of Come, Lord Jesus. The audience can also participate in this response.)
APPLE:	Like sweet fruit, you feed God's people.
RESPONSE:	Come, Lord Jesus.
RAINBOW:	You are a sign of God's promise.
RESPONSE:	Come, Lord Jesus.
STARS:	Those who love you are as many as the stars in the sky.

RESPONSE: Come, Lord Jesus.

TAMBOURINE: We will sing to you and praise you forever.
RESPONSE: Come, Lord Jesus.

GRAPES: As grapes give wine, so you give joy.
RESPONSE: Come, Lord Jesus.

SCROLL: You are God's word, promising freedom.
RESPONSE: Come, Lord Jesus.

ROSE: You are Mary's son.
RESPONSE: Come, Lord Jesus.

CARPENTER'S
     TOOLS: You were a child in Joseph's home.
RESPONSE: Come, Lord Jesus.

MANGER: Blessed Jesus, once a baby in Bethlehem:
RESPONSE: Come, Lord Jesus.

End

About the Authors

Randi Goldstein has been a theatre professional for more than ten years. As the Artistic Director of a children's theatre in New York, she directed more than a dozen shows for children, and developed workshops for young people interested in careers in the arts. During her time as the Director of Operations for an East Coast lighting and sound company, she provided support for shows for literally hundreds of schools, churches, and libraries, as well as national tours, and concerts for major recording artists. She is a member of Actors' Equity Association, has degrees in Psychology and Theatre, and is currently pursuing a Master of Fine Arts degree in Theatre Management.

Dina Strong worked with young children for more than a decade as storyteller, teacher and children's literature specialist before becoming a writer and editor of story-based educational materials in 1987. She has a degree in Literature, with a minor in Education, and has worked with children in groups whose numbers ranged from four to a hundred. Spindle Press has published three of her previous titles: *The Vineyard and the Wedding: Four Stories of God's Kingdom, Many Miles to Bethlehem: Stories of Advent and Christmas* and *Hosanna and Alleluia: Stories of Holy Week and Easter.*

Notes

Notes

Notes

Notes

Notes